The *N-WORD* Revisited

Racism in 21st Century America

by

Henry L. N. Anderson, B.S.Ed., M.A.R.,
Ed.D., Ph.D., LL.D., D.D., Litt.D., Th.D., L.H.D.

Foreword by
Rev. Marilyn Rose Franck Glenn, B.S., M.A., D.Min.
Pastoral Psychotherapist

First Printing, January 2017. Revised Second Printing, March 2017 (Selected references included)

Published by
Enigami & Rednow Publishers, New York
www.EnigamiRednow.com
ISBN: 1945674040
ISBN-13 9781945674044

DEDICATION

To the memory of Robert Hall and Lou Smith, community organizers, programs creators, and administrators of indigenous services, and...

To all whose lives were given—or taken—black and white—in the struggles down through the years...that they shall not have suffered and died in vain, and...

To Patrick Blair, age 19 who promised me he'd be right back...thirty minutes before he was killed in a drive by shooting two blocks from his home.

"It was Msumongu, Msumongu who had no hate for any man, who said: 'What I fear is that one day, when they are turned to loving, they will find that we are turned to hating!'"

–Alan Paton, author of *Cry, the Beloved Country*

TABLE OF CONTENTS

FOREWORD

I am honored to be asked to write the Foreword for this second book on racism by Dr. Henry L. N. Anderson. We met while we were graduate students in theological seminaries in 1958. That was the decade that this country was just awakening to the issues of discrimination in education and other institutions. "Andy," as he was known then, and I had no contact for 58 years, until August, 2016 when Google connected us again. I welcome the opportunity to join with the man who wrote and published *You and Race—A Christian Reflects* (1960).

His message has not changed. He still advocates for the brotherhood of mankind and for the individual responsibility that we have to do more than just get along, as Rodney King pleaded. When asked, "Do you think the [race] problem will ever be completely solved?" he responded in his 1960 book: "'Ever' is a very long time, isn't it? (Still, it might take forever, even forever!) Seriously, I don't think the big problem will be completely solved. The big problem is not race prejudice but human sin. I see no quick end to that. So, even if the day comes when there will be little racial injustice, there will still remain a great deal of human injustice…. However, it will be left to people like you and me to help reduce the amount of this type of human injustice."

An astute social observer and analyst, Dr. Anderson is a man of faith who offers the reader a passionate, informed, and well-researched review of the meaning of racism in America in all of its many manifestations, obvious and unseen, known and unknown, recognized and unrecognized by us. He points out that everyone who lives in American society—black, white, and all other ethnic groups—is deeply impacted by institutionalized racism in housing, in employment, in education, in the legal system, in sports, in entertainment, in healthcare, in psychological well-being, in financial opportunity, in equal protection, and in respect of personhood.

Next follows a hard and revealing look at the *N-WORD*, from its historic roots in black slavery. He gets our attention by showing the blatant disrespect for black life; and reminds us that we face a hundred years of personal commitment and dedicated effort, after we acknowledge our personal racist character. He pulls our human options from the words of his late friend, The Rev. Dr. Martin Luther King, Jr.: "We will have to learn to live together as brothers; or we will perish together as fools."

Dr. Anderson warns us that road ahead is critically important, and will not be easy. Racism (the disadvantages and denials of fuller life opportunities) will not go away tomorrow—not even in a hundred years of tomorrows. But, the author projects an absolute imperative for a rebirth to take place in our collective consciousness that will lead to deliberate and effective changes, so that more Americans can benefit from living in an enlightened and universally fair and equitable society.

I believe that the urgency is now. We are at a crucial juncture in our country's history when racial injustice is reaching fever pitch.

We must commit to changing our basic assumptions and behaviors, and must pledge to continue to be proactive in bringing about the kind of society we desire.

Rev. Marilyn Rose Franck Glenn, B.S., M.A., D.Min.,
Pastoral Psychotherapist

PREFACE

Robert Hall and Lou Smith were the co-organizers of a neighborhood services program in Watts, California in the 1960's. Using their own—and very little—money, these two "brothers" opened the doors of their facility and started teaching "whatever a sistah and a brother needed to, or wanted to learn." The organization soon caught roots, attracted local political and community support and provided a unique array of "life and living services" for every level of a depressed community, year in and year out.

This writer was one of the many individual supporters who made his personal talents and resources available to the operation that called itself OPERATION BOOTSTRAP (because our people need to pull themselves up by their own bootstraps!).

When Robert Hall died suddenly of a heart attack, I penned the poem below (which was published by a students' group at California State University, Los Angeles):

THE GOOD DO DIE

Robert Hall was a good nigger. He was, like me, from Georgia. He was a nigger lover. He even said the word like it was some sort of 400-year-old poem, spoken by a 400-year-old poet. Nigger Africa. Nigger from Africa. Nigger who wanted to go back to Africa before he died. Nigger who said to me very recently: "Andy, baby, I am tired…you hear me…tired. Niggers got me tired…Niggers-a-kill you."

Yes, Robert Hall, niggers-a-kill you. But you know love is that way, Robert. You knew early in the game that you can't love niggers unless they can kill you. You knew all along, Robert, how much heart you got to have, to know, to feel, to care about niggers. You knew, Robert. You had to. Robert, good-nigger-friend, what brings such heavy tears to my eyes is the memory of your soft, tired, concerned voice—just over a month ago when you poured your heart out to me. All you wanted—"Getting to be an old nigger now,"—was to go back home to "the big-foot country and settle down…not run any more…not have to deal with niggers: with painful, deep-seated, terrible, city-nigger problems." You wanted so little, nigger. Robert, I cannot hold back the tears (Robert, I just cried like a motherfucker…hey! Man, couldn't help myself!). Read

about your ass in the paper, man: You dead and gone!
All the way back to White Plains, New York. How
could a nigger black as you come from anything white?
You right baby, blackness is no color. You right man,
blackness is loving niggers. Go on baby, I ain't cryin'
no more for you now. For you, Robert, I'm going to
keep on loving niggers 'till they kill my ass, too!

Love, Andy baby.

INTRODUCTION

I was watching CNN, on the 2016 Presidential campaign; and Don Lemon was "apologizing for the existence and the ugliness of the 'word' now disguised as the 'N-WORD.'" At least, that is how I heard what he said. For sure, there is "ugliness"…some of the ugliest ugliness, over a period of five hundred years that the human race could produce! But, that ugliness should not be hidden or concealed; no, it cannot be covered over sugar-coated and its persistent dehumanizing effects should not be minimized in any way. Both must be acknowledged. That's how we start to heal; and I will tell you why. We, Americans are born into racism.

My next thoughts were words I learned (and memorized) some seventy years ago! The 23rd Psalm (King James Version): "The Lord is my Shepherd; I shall not want. He maketh me to lie down in green pastures: he leadeth me beside the still waters. He restoreth my soul: he leadeth me in the paths of righteousness for his name's sake. Yea, though I walk through the valley of the shadow of death, I will fear no evil: for thou art with me; thy rod and thy staff they comfort me. Thou preparest a table before me in the presence of mine enemies: thou anointh my head with oil; my cup runneth over. Surely goodness and mercy shall follow me all the days of my life: and I will dwell in the house of the Lord for ever." (Thomas Nelson Inc., Nashville, Camden, New York, 1972)

That passage from the Book of Psalms, somehow allowed me to co-exist with my impression that the Bible does not condemn slavery but views it like one of several social strata in existence at various times, and that the institution of slavery is a reality for humans to figure out the best way they can. Clearly, my impression was that slavery was seen as a social class, with rights and limitations, not unlike other classes, below the upper classes. Yet, I know with all of my being and beliefs that the Message of the Bible does repeat a clear and expressed rejection of slavery, or the utter disdain for the horrors of human pain and suffering over five hundred years, here in America: 500 years of inflicting pain and suffering that continues today and that defines racism.

I now write a proclamation of a piece of reoccurring human history. It is a reminder of the pending human need. Irrespective of an individual's sensitivity to the use of the N-

WORD, the following discussion must happen; and it appears God has assigned the task to me…and to you. I will do my best to deliver; and where I get stuck—if I do—I will reach out to you, to some of you, to you who will be sought out for input, if not already.

First, however, I shall ask that we pause for a few moments in silence…. During the silence I saw flashes of abuse, and torture, and rape and pillage, and terror and pain—fear, and bleeding and hurting, and burning, and rejection, and insult, and neglect, and dying—even crying, and pleading, and praying, and hoping, and killing, and suicide, and hating, and hurting, and burning, and lynching, and terrorizing, and killing, and shooting, and beating, and even cutting, and scalding, and poisoning, and murdering, and neglecting, and cursing, and disrespecting, and hating, and demoralizing, and deceiving, discrediting, denying, discriminating, betraying, and distorting, lying, and mistreating, outlawing, and prejudging; misguidance, and malediction, also amortizing the health and wholesomeness of humans by the thousands, treating them as animals—or worse—as property, as objects of pleasure or entertainment, and as measures of wealth and evidence of superiority. Then I said a silent "Amen; to God be the glory…."

SECTION ONE

Everything horrible that you can imagine, every violent act that can be forced upon a human being, the cruelest of treatment or violence that ever could be imagined, this is but a small part of what the *N-WORD* embalms, represents, references, and institutionalizes. It is a picture of rape in the middle of the night—or in broad daylight—with other children hearing every movement and sound, every grieving outcry, every prayer and wish to die, every cry for God to do something, please...and do it now!

The *N-WORD* label allows generations of the descendants of violators to revisit the past, by way of subtle reminders that the dastardly deeds have been done, and continue to bear economic advantage for the oppressing racial bloc as a reminder—and a warning—blackness is not valued, is undervalued, is assigned measured value and by no means will be allowed to compete on fair, let alone on equal economic planes. The *N-WORD* is a symbol, a code, a clear and present warning to not step out of line, less corrective action will restrain—even punish those who do not seem to remember the meaning of the *N-WORD*. This is your history, not *his*. It speaks to no other history. It does not remember the Holocaust, or the Crusades, or the opium purges in China, nor man's inhumanity to man wherever in the world, at whatever times in human history.

Black persons were the slaves; black persons were beaten and forced to meet every human desire, at whatever the cost to them and others who looked like them. Blacks were not valued very much; they were expendable; they were chattel; and they remain the wounded offspring of wounded fore-parents, of wounded ancestral lines, of generations urging deliberate amelioration, with a strong sense of urgency. We are the surviving embodiment of our fallen ancestors. We are the reminder of what it used to be like; we are the reminder that the offspring of the slave abuser and murderer, cannot take such pleasures from blacks in this day and time. But he tries; he wants to know and to experience what his fore-fathers engaged. He tries but he can't know the gory details and must summon up traditional props—the *N-WORD* brings him close, as close as he can get. He is no fool; he knows you are not your fore-parents. People of color will not be his slave—ever again.

So people of color must be controlled by insult, by mistreatment, by oppression, by abuse under the color of law; by private membership exclusions, and restrictive patterns of housing and worshipping; by restrictions and limitations to educational opportunities—as reminders in every way possible. Real estate segregates the living environments; direct, subtle, and programmed discrimination controls who gets hired, retained, promoted, discharged, or becomes a part of corporate. Children are separated in neighborhood schools, even when busing is the effective vehicle. Access to better foods, better water, better community amenities, proximity to commercial outlets, cultural establishments, recreational outlets. Equal protection under the law is denied, and the criminal correctional system is operated without justice to people of color. There is, indeed, a one-word symbol for all of this!

The *N-WORD* is peddled as a commercial commodity. It is peddled like a baseball card, collecting value as it reminds and establishes: in our national consciousness there have been no apologies, no retribution, no repentance, no grieving, no compensation or reparations, no attempt to fess up or even explain that the nature and extent of misdeeds—of actions so cruel and unreal that only computer games can possibly match or top the level of violence and horror; that the *N-WORD* codifies and represents all of this in the history of the United States of America. And, America stands alone….

The *N-WORD* confirms a social commitment to deny and excuse the horrors and brutality pelted out upon persons of color and others so misfortunate—especially urban youth, teens and young people who encounter rookie cops too frequently; and my fifteen year old granddaughter, Nellicia, agrees. But, the inner city presents a much larger opportunity: Her older brother, Patrick, complained to his father, to his uncle (who is a policeman) and to me that he was often harassed by one officer in particular, at the playground where he played basketball. Each of us proposed reporting and discussing the incidents with senior officials. Patrick disagreed.

Opportunities were missed for sure: The harassing officer was part of a gang detail, and he/she might have informed, warned or suggested to the parents, who were new to the neighborhood, that Patrick might be drawn toward gang affiliation, especially during the two "permitted" home searches (looking for contraband) officers requested of, and were reluctantly granted by Patrick's parents. Of course the police officers knew more than they shared; but, a more open or communal interface might have suggested actions we all might have taken. Patrick was killed in a drive-by shooting at about 2:30PM on the eve of his mother's birthday, April 13, 2015 (also the birthday of my 102 year old mother-in-law).

The estrangement between families and police is rooted in the our history of racism.

When black families in the inner-cities of America share their stories of "having police in for breakfast," we will see and feel and know committed citizens have pledged to help save our nation. First, we must save our children; that will allow us to save ourselves; and we thereby save America. Racism is not a death sentence. However, I totally reject callous indifference and/or any sibilance of the notion that black people have no rights that white people are bound to respect. ***Too many Patricks have been sacrificed; and it may be time now to consider withholding lethal weapons from community police officers***. Swat teams are readily available when, and as needed.

American society has evolved from a system so cruel and inhumane, the violence and ugliness of sexual and human life violations so extreme and perverted that no civilized society would ever excuse such behavior if, in fact, there is any real belief in God among these people who were the perpetrators of the violence. The *N-WORD* is proof positive that there were hundreds of years of dastardly deeds and it is taking hundreds of years for justice or retribution to be hinted at, let alone being imposed by the same Hands of God.

Put differently, in American society a 500-year perception and relationship evolved into and through a sadistic and deadly cruel system of suppression and human deprivation, violence the level of which no humans could survive without also losing mental capacity and spiritual tenacity. History has recorded such human meanness; the perpetrators survive and thrive while the victims are hardly remembered as human beings.

The *N-WORD* is a reminder—no, a message, a statement, a confirmation that the tradition of violence against blacks—also by blacks—is alive and well, and is thriving and looking to grow—in –Chicago, in Los Angeles, in New York, in New Orleans and Atlanta, in Birmingham, and in Tyler, Texas (where domino players live to be over 100 years old!)—wherever black people remain pushed up against each other, crowded into confining quarters, forced into unemployment for lack of access to jobs or job locations, or the opportunity for gainful employment, coupled with a focus on petty crime prevention and adjudication, whether real or potential, part of a campaign to keep the *N-WORD* in his place. This is a societal objective, a mandated character of a social order which is historically and psychologically preferred as suitable for the *N-WORD* culture and sub-culture.

What everyone needs to confront is that 500 years of slave marketing created an attitude, a choice of values, a system of denial and exclusion, a lifestyle, system of government and cultural value system that begins with being white. That gave rise to the system of preference and exclusive right for whites to dominate, control and receive the bulk of the benefits of society, whether by civilized or by uncivilized procedures, subsystems, and deadly behaviors even being not out of character.

Professional sports, especially football, mimics the very ownership and control system that sustained the

institution of slavery during all its direct years, and since has defined the after-slavery-years. We are dealing with a monster—not a school child. RACISM should always be written in capital letters…and so should the *N-WORD*. They embody the prevailing, constant, and enveloping presence and reality of an unequal playing field, of an impossible option: TO BE TREATED EQUALLY. Realistically, it is not happening…yet; in fact, it cannot happen overnight no matter what force declares, "Let it be done!"

Black people who can stomach the *N-WORD* are in denial; but I don't mean that negatively or as you might think in a social context. The denial about which I speak is the historic ugly. One word—only one word—in the annals of American history—only this one word can recall all of the murder, all of the rape, all of the terror, all of the torture, all of the pain, all of the desperation, all of the suffering, all of the neglect deliberately channeled to entire black families, lines and futures—all of which fostered hate, so real, so powerful, so endorsed, so precise upon a reality that was preferred, that is preferred, that will yet be prevalent—all cleverly and effectively costumed, hidden from view, distracting and concealing all the shit that history has wrapped in its pants legs, and that current day magicians camouflage behind the becoming more acceptable smoke screen, the *N-WORD*.

In Mood Poetry for Everyone—In An Age of Rap (Conquering Books, LLC, Charlotte, NC, 2006, p. 261) I **called** it "Sweet Illusion…"

SWEET ILLUSION

My heart seeks to be or not: to know its destiny. My heart cries out with a hurting seal that ponders its own echoes. My heart sleeps and rejoices in its own troubled dreams. And by itself stumbles through the passing of the day:

Its rhythm flowing like chaotic thunders. And by itself finds periodic glimpses of what all knowledge discerns is absent. And by itself laughs to its own resounding lies that keep it in sweet illusion.

Yet awhile it faintly moves: then again trembles long; but ends it now in uproar. Yet awhile this state reigns in perfect acceptance: A tender air of narcissism—even so in contamination. Yet awhile it introspects, then quickly drinks to intoxication from its own illusory potion.

What a lie my heart conceals, and from itself first of all: a dripping, sinking into void. What a life its entire campaign, a decided deception with a self-giving royal welcome. What a lie it feeds itself, and swells to a swollen ugliness— finding still primitive satisfaction.

Can this thing in me not use some rational substance to calm itself from its own turmoil? Can this thing, this unseemly manner cast away—not simply pretend it has, but has not? Can this thing in me, this heart that pumps and drinks its own contents, not find an adequate spring?

I must ask because I bear its weight, a heavy moving sting; a slowly creeping, then rapid-laughing fiend. I must ask that I might help it see the unreality in which it lives, in which no essence be. I must ask because it's me, and mine this heart that feeds on lies; ask, but answer none I find.

"What a lie my heart confesses—and of itself first of all," failing to see the dark and damning images of a deliberate past, a determined present, and a dedicated future. Racism of the oldest version; racism in its deepest grooves; racism in its most subtle settlements; racism in its most highly sophisticated entrenchments, interwoven in all aspects of social existence—this, all of this, is what the *N-WORD* disguises at its best, and represents at its worst—nearly wide open before our eyes.

Young neighborhood children hear the word itself: loudly and often, in various combinations, to various friends and relatives, homeys and sistah girls, and people from my set. Teens and talented ones refer to current events and daily conditions, to recalled events and past pains, fears and unforgiving moments, and days , and weeks and years, and events too gross to be recalled. And all of this is but a part of what they know, and it is all covered and camouflaged by the inventive N-WORD. Our human dilemma is relatively simple, really: The N-WORD epitomizes the hard, cold, truth that RACISM exists and is old; it is a cruel and critical lien or mortgage on our future here in the United States of America; and it is the single-most serious variable to our survival as a perpetual nation, at whatever political level we would aspire to enjoy and perpetuate. I think the words of my old friend and brother, The Rev. Dr. Martin Luther King, Jr., speak well what I am here saying:

"Either we learn to live together as brothers, or we will perish together as fools."

And our actions must be mental and physical and real and mutual, and total. And, we can do this; as humans we can do it.

Decent people, and teachers, church people and preachers, white people and black—alike—say this abbreviated word—not as the deception it is but as the social tonic, the appeasement of a corrupt social order, infested with an historic stink that will take long to fix because the heirs to the huge inhumane financial gains prefer to recall only the upside—their side, the generations removed from the scene of

the crimes. They applaud grandpa for his thoughtfulness, and for his financial genius—not for his participation in the dirtiest and most deadly campaign of man's inhumanity to man since the Crusades or Egyptian era.

Rappers and artists and entrepreneurs try to accommodate the social inequity and may experience phenomenal financial success but find they do not—cannot escape the insidious racial mantra which is the suppressed reality that is felt deep down inside, and is overtly acknowledged, by both viewers—those whose lives are linked to the creation and evolution of the racism system and those whose mothers were raped and preferred and by those whose fathers were enslaved and dehumanized by a heavy challenge that demanded submission or death. These are but some of the historical contexts of the *N-WORD*.

Here are two versions of the black man's story (Anderson, *Mood Poetry, In An Age of Rap*, Conquering Books LLC, Charlotte, NC, 2006):

AFRICA AND BACK

At the village of my father,
With my mother busy there,
I learned the skills of a warrior
And the habits of the red deer.

I watched my mother prepare for
Market, weaving straw, rolling clay;
And Granny stood beside her, watching
Her weave her way.

All the cousins of my village
Seemed to know Ashanti art;
Yet, for them life was simple,
And everyone did his part.
In my youth, there came a strange one,
Bringing barrels of 'pink coconut milk.'
I saw the village celebration,
With our women wearing silk.

When the drumming dances ended,
Men were laid all out to rest.
But when morning came to see us,
Many relatives had gone 'West.'

Both my father and my mother
Must have joined the band;
For I searched for them all over—
In the forest and on the sea sand.

Somehow, I sensed a feeling when
My crippled Uncle Kwasi cried;
There was an anguish in his deep eyes—
An expression I saw before, when his father died.

Now the people talked strange talk;
Of many things so foreign to hear;
While drums of distant cousins
Tell of a gripping, newly felt fear.

With youthful daring, I chased behind them—
Some small tears in my eyes;
By the water I found a sweat cloth,
At once recognizing my father's dyes.

So I returned home to my village:
An instant man had come of age!

The slave traders would come again
Told the face of our village sage.

Early one morning, with 'pops and bangs,'
White faces came with metal spears.
They forced the strong and the young
Into long work-gangs.

This time, I made the journey
Through miles of jungle bush,
Until finally weary and near exhaustion,
We fell down from a push.

The rooms were dark and damp and dingy;
The air had urine smell.
At once I knew the fate that was my mother's,
Felt the blood where my father fell!

To keep alive became my secret...
To see the journey through.
Many others mourned in sadness...
Some saw death as noble, too.

From a deep, dark hole in urine-wet clay—
Chained man to man—
We fell onto a wooden floor of
A sea-going vessel one day.

There began a sojourn four hundred years long:
Out to the world, and back…
To survive and multiply on every continent,
To build a black, genetic tract!

Until the return to Mother Africa,
When all black slavery shall be spent…
I come back, 400 years later, to this damp
Dark hole and its urine scent….

TWILIGHT OF A BLACK ERA

So many ships ago…
In quest of fortunes

A journey—endless—
Was begun in Africa.

Thus began a plot too
Cunning for the 'plotters!"

The black genes of Africa
Began their world conquest.

Now, on nearly every continent,
'Blackness' is prominent.

Heavy is the imprint of
Black Africa on the world.

Evolution is draped in blackness,
While journalists record 'revolution.'

God—secretly—must be fair,
And History Her mascot!

Life in the world becomes at once
A poem and a streak of light!

O, to look—as God—
Upon the course of man!

Shudder, O Man, in
Your finite projections;

For a trick has been played
On the world;
History whispers in my ear:
"Mankind is turning Black!"

SECTION TWO

When *"**Africa and Back**"* was first read, readers became saddened and showed great emotion. It was clearly painful for them. So painful, in fact, that in no time flat, I penned the broader, more philosophical ending of the next to the last stanza: "…to survive and multiply on every continent, to build a black genetic tract!"

Immediately, upon sharing that brief summation, a radical mood change occurred, and it could be clearly seen! God did not *punish* black people by their becoming slaves during a savage period of inhuman history. *What God really did was select the black gene to re-seed all continents on the earth.* Maybe the Bible does not condemn slavery…?

Urban teens, inner-city encased young people, and urban young men (especially) and women freely exchange the traditional salutation. They say the *N-WORD* to each other, with each other, about one another, and will use the term to express a third person's perspective, regardless of race or gender. They all seem to cling to the word— almost as if in preparation of a pending event or attack during which the word would be cast at them, from and by those who do not represent a redemptive social attitude.

They clearly speak their message: "We are the victims of victims, but are not defined by their legacy."

They can, will and must make their own way, such that the rest of the world wants to follow—these survivors—with pants on their asses, messages in gestures, words so coupled as to rhyme and chime—setting for all to see an N-WORD descendant, a capable defendant, a realistic, aware, and knowledgeable heir to a damnable legacy. Hell, yeah, you know who you are, even though you were not there: to feel the pain, to see the cruelty; to have to swallow and digest the damning pain, and all the terror and the rest.

You could not defend your ancestors nor now reverse the pain. But you can, will, and must let the fucked up world know you are in tune with the family historic trust. You must continue to perfect your tendency to lead, and inspire, to set new standards and break all records in every phase of our corporate lives:

basketball, science, tennis, golf, track, field, soccer, business, hockey, art, performance, medicine, entertainment, boxing, etc., etc., in lifestyle and fashion, in human caring and passion. Yes, you are the offspring of your ancestors, and it is yours to lead, to create, to dominate the imaginations for generations to come. You are to confirm the commitment and the progress and to acknowledge the meaning of the *N-Word*, and the realistic joint commitment to reverse its 500-year impact.

Thus, the *N-WORD* is best defined as the specific reference to the cruelty perpetrated upon blacks—women, children, men, grandmothers, grandfathers, relatives, friends, and strangers—during 500 years of mistreatment, subjugation, mental deprivation, cultural stagnation, spiritual castration, educational deferment, and all the horrors of 500 years of domination, to the will and pleasure of an unhealthy class of humans who still refuse to stop—even curtail—their un-Godly sophisticated and structured systems that deny fair and equal but reinforce and perpetuate unfair and unequal opportunities even to dream of life, liberty, and the pursuit of happiness within the context of American society. This remains shameful.

The *N-WORD* is not a reference to black people; it is **a reference to the treatment** of black people, starting about the year 1490-1492 but gaining momentum in the years following 1492, in Virginia, United States of America. In that year, as with many others, black people were brought to the Western Hemisphere, some as purchased chattels, some as captured individuals—all bound and chained, and brought to America (those who survived the long and arduous trip and treatment). And they were indistinguishable from those black aborigines who had occupied these lands 12,000 before Columbus fumbled upon the North American continent. Black people are Washitaw; and earth is their homeland. Black people are the ancestral lineage of all races on earth. Or, so scientists promulgate.

SECTION THREE

The Sound of a Word.

Is it beginning now to sound like a dirty word? Like an unhealthy misadventure? Are you beginning to see the self-deception by both camps: the racist inheritors and the slave heirs who still wait for reparations—a word too small to cover what it represents. Yet, no single word or code in the English language encases more historic turbulence than does the *N-WORD*.

Sociopaths, racial bigots, victims favoring historic racism, and victims committed to reversing the character of our racist society are in a tug of war. The chief advocates are those on the offending end of racism. People enjoying the daily benefits of being on top, in the preferred class, are not preoccupying themselves with the daily doses of unfair and decidedly biased treatment and neglect meted out minute by minute on the underclass, the last to be hired, if hired at all. But what makes us all victims is time. What we face as a race-based social order did not evolve over one or even several generations. This type of relating, specifically to the United States of America was born some 500 years ago. Why it started or how it started are irrelevant now. Our dilemma is that it is going to take years to reverse or to even significantly impact the negative character of American society, as it is fueled by historic racism. Though not remotely possible, even if 95% of our society wanted to see an early end to the extensive inequities, it is likely to take not less than another 100 years to see evidence of effective changes.

A Time Remembered.

I just buried my mother-in-law; she was 102 years old. When we sat and talked about how it was growing up stuff she said could make you sick to your stomach. Or, by assuming her perspective, these recall sessions showed progress…that things were constantly getting better. Surely, she was correct: all aspects of the treatments of blacks and other minorities became a lot less outrageous, and much more tolerable. Each adjustment in the harshness and severity of maltreatment does suggest a kind of progress. Less physical and psychological pain does help mitigate the effects of increased emotional and spiritual pain. Her sons—and all the sons and daughters of other mothers and fathers— know first hand, and from their own measured existence, what a living hell they struggle to exist in: to find decent support for themselves, later for their wives, and then for their families. Is this ingratitude? No, absolutely not. One cannot be either grateful or ungrateful for the manifestations of the racist character of our national lifestyle. It is our inheritance. It is our American legacy.

Impatience brought on by a sudden revelation or epiphany only pushes such persons over toward the behavior of the sociopath. That is so because racism is racial hatred; it is a passion, an emotional and sociological conditioning that defines our values, that exposes our character. It is a sociological conditioning that cannot be stamped out by a sudden passion, or gesture, or repenting action. Results will take time, for any of us: for all of us!

Self-proclaiming bigots will have to convert, from being believers in the correctness of segregated lifestyles and isolated living quarters and sections of town and of social intercourse. But, in addition, the adjusted cost of fair play, of leveling the playing field are more than common or ordinary sensibilities will normally tolerate. So, we have put our society in the state of imbalance we cannot quickly extricate ourselves from no matter what we do, or how we do it. *But, here is the real deal: We have spent 500 years building an unequal social structure which threatens our long term existence.* And even if we find a way to commit to changing our society, to opening it up to what is equally fair, we are looking at a century-long campaign, to begin with. Thus, the victim and the victimizer can conspire and collectively promote equalizing behaviors and attitudes. Love and social practices will have to change before our eyes, and at our own hands. We will have to arrest the *N-WORD* references.

American social life is contaminated and one segment of society continues to pay an unredeemable price. Of course, it is unequal; it is also costly—seeing lives begin and end—without ever adjusting the account. There is no equity; the imbalance is too great, and it increases. RACISM has a grip on our lives, on our society, and on our future. It remains the essential ingredient in the political gumbo of America's projection toward an ideal of democracy.

America's future—and her maximum quality of life—are inextricably linked to how the historic evils of Jim Crow and RACISM are managed. One major start is to impose by adoption and general practice this corrective couplet: CAPITAL SOCIAL CRIMES should be met by CAPITAL SOCIAL PUNISHMENTS. The short summary is reliable. The construct takes benefits out of public displays of racist acts. No one can benefit financially, nor continue an existing financially beneficial lifestyle by virtue of blatant or by public displays of RACISM.

We need not and cannot hide our personal biases—pro or con—by dignifying the abbreviated symbol, the *N-WORD*. Our fate is set; we extricate ourselves by dedicated, deliverable actions. Our commitment must be for at least one hundred years going forward. Either we do it or we don't. We decide; our future is inextricably linked to the quality of future we will have...if we make it.

Perhaps, it is fitting to make a declarative statement: These contents are not special but they are specific. They refer to one historic and specific scenario—the historic evolution and current dynamics of racism—the institution of racism in America. This is not about the Holocaust and historic maltreatment of the Jewish people. These remembrances are not recalls of human sex trafficking and child slavery and sexual exploitation. These, too, are unique social plagues; and, there are more, many more and they exist in many parts of the world. That, notwithstanding, this writing is dedicated to recalling grievous descriptions of hundreds of years of orchestrated inequity that defines the scope of existence of black Americans.

Not ordained by God, the full character and persona of a superior race dominating as they should an inferior race (of almost human beings) was, surely believed to be—or was—ordained by God, Himself. Why else, and how else could such a state of affairs persist for some five hundred years? Subsequent generations participated largely in passive ways, relative to the economic disparity within current American society. However, as everyone knows, the absence of diversity means no economic parity; no social parity; no cultural parity; no psychological parity; and no educational parity. An offspring from a slave person's history or heritage is dogged and disadvantaged from inception to the grave! This is so because it is so. An *N-WORD*'s life represents no rights which a slave master's descendants are bound to honor and respect. For levity, while this state of affairs is bound not to last through eternity, it can continue to poison interracial equal opportunity for another hundred years or more. This is not a short-sighted, biased prejudgment upon a class of people, or upon the component of people; it is simply true. RACISM is alive and well; and let no one of us fail to acknowledge this fact!

The pattern of RACISM seems to be that it thrives and re-roots in the fertile social order of newer generations of young Americans who sup upon the fertility of their parent generations, themselves self-indulgent and shortness of vision—not to mention hardness of heart and total neglect of effort, of understanding, or of conscious commitment to love thy neighbor as thyself. People who are identified, labeled, and presumed to be subjects known to be identified by the *N-WORD* also face the challenge. If your father was enslaved by my father it does not exempt your required commitment to embrace and implement the love thy neighbor as thyself rule.

SECTION FOUR

So help me God...the destiny of America is co-dependent upon the eradication of public and private—racism. Whether black or white, racial intolerance and unequal opportunity will continue to reduce America's status in the world, and it will jeopardize the role America is best trained to play in effecting the delicate balance of racial harmony in a violent and desperate world, leaning hard toward religious intolerance, then full scale war of conflicting religious ideologies! Who will speak to cousins in Iraq, who kill cousins in Iran? Who will mediate when Syria declares war on Afghanistan? Are you aware? Do you know how the energy of the *N-WORD* resonates in the blood streams of people whose lives represent no rights that the opposition is bound to respect?

Personal histories, historic recollections of my generation hardships, narrow misses, and failures to survive are too real and precious to discard from the individual memory bank. And in these recalled scenarios of survival, some of the ugliest of human misconduct is relived and remembered and revalued. But, you and I are decent citizens, fair-minded adults who responsibly participate in the unfolding drama of a free and open society, one structured by the greatest self-directing document on the face of the earth—the Constitution of the United States of America (in Assembly).

Of the history of slavery in America, we acknowledge its reality. The incipient horrors of that condition we have heard about, read about, have seen pictures—movies and documentaries—we have a pretty good idea of what that awful period was like. And even if you don't truly know the horror, we are willing to tolerate acknowledged dirty language and salutations, verbally violent descriptions and references, painful and hurting descriptions, as we endure mental and emotional trauma, as we witness cruel and ugly characterization—by children to children, by adults to children, by adults to adults, professional to professional, athlete to athlete, woman to woman, youth to youth, man to man, Rappers to us all. Are we listening? Can we go forward, cuddling the symbol, disguising the reality, and ignoring the urgency? And are you nearly aware of our lack of understanding of either the urgency or of the magnitude of the task before us: the neutralization of racism in American society?

SECTION FIVE

Recognizing Christian (Religious) Racism

It reoccurs to my consciousness that **The Holy Bible does not condemn slavery**, the institution of slavery; nor does The Bible declare an unequivocal zero tolerance for human beings being owned by other human beings, as are animals and other portable, non-human chattel is owned.

But let me pause briefly to define and clarify these very familiar terms we are considering. Racism, as we might all agree is holding to the notion that one person is preferred, is better, is more worthy, is more blessed, is more human, is more desirable, is more to be favored than another, primarily based on racial differences. That's pretty clear, pretty simple; but, it is absolutely true…for all Americans. No living person, either here in America or elsewhere, really, is immune from the contagion of racism. Racism is like the air we breathe, or the water that we drink, or even like the food that we eat. Just as we need air, food, and water to survive, while we survive, we do so from the foundation of racism, as our essential and critical spring board to what we call today, civilized co-existence.

As we all know, or at least might concur with, every human cruelty conceivable is as much a part of slavery as the smell is a part of human feces. Why should we pretend? Why should we want to excuse, ignore, or separate the smell from the feces? Do not laugh at the question. It is a serious reality—not even a question—for Christianity. Unless you can locate what I could not find, a matter-of-fact, no nonsense declaration in The Holy Bible, which unequivocally rejects (condemns, absolutely forbids, repudiates) the classism we refer to as racism, it partially explains how this racial attitude, lifestyle, and state of being characterizes and defines the true nature of our co-existence. We are all victims.

And, there is no quid pro quo available. In other words, we (all of us whether bastard or saint) are subject to our historic dilemma. As such, we will remain racists, even if-, when-, and while we decide to work toward making this world a better place, to borrow from our heritage. In America, we can easily claim the past 500 years as the conditioning period during which our present state of racism has evolved. Like it or not; accept it or reject it; it remains our reality. So, our options have been paraphrased by a most human American, the Rev. Dr. Martin Luther King, Jr., who put it this way for us: *"We must learn to live together as brothers, or we will perish together as fools!"*

Frankly, I am ready to try it. I've been ready since I became aware—of our common reality! I am racist because I am; I could be nothing else growing up in a culture and tradition and existence that is what it is. Denials do not help; and they do not change anything. Just like me, you—each of you reading and/or contemplating this dynamic must face your own mirror. And, you tell me who is looking back and what that says to you. And, one other point worthy of mentioning: your racism is not the same as mine—and there are other kinds. Yours, for example, might be aggressive or protracted racism, coming from the deepest, historic roots of the color distinction. Mine, on the other hand might be defensive racism—my trying to survive and thrive as best I can, given your advantages and my disadvantages. Then, there is what we might call evolving racism, where newborns (with no other environmental options) must grow up in this world, that time and circumstance have created for them....

Perhaps, now they can epitomize the following poem (You *and* Race—A Christian Reflects, Anderson, 1960):

A COLORLESS GLOW

My home has become a tiny cage,
Around which people stand in rage.
They put me here, out of their way,
Yet, come to watch me every day.
They do not trust even the bars
That they have made to glow as stars.
And this is why they keep me here:
They see not the 'Glow;' and they fear!

Prior to now, I walked the streets—
A common man with common speech.
All was well 'til I stopped a man,
And asked if I might shake his hand?
His face was brown, and this I know;
But, as I shook, I saw him glow.
There was not light—no, none at all:
Just his color, I saw it fall.

Excitedly, I ran to tell
All the world what I beheld.
At every door, I turned in sheen;
For those folks, too, had surely seen!
Wherever I stopped to tell my tale,
I found no color there to hail.

Hard to believe, yet it was so:
Everybody had a colorless glow.

Alas, I turned to thank my God
For making our lives much less hard.
For, all men then could be as One:
A colorless glow as God's Son.
I offered my life for his use,
To bring all hearts into His noose.
Indeed I knew that God did this
To help all men encounter bliss.

I gave a smile to every man—
To a little boy who turned and ran.
I laughed at him in all my joy,
But thought not twice about the boy.
I came upon a crippled man, and
Asked if I might shake his hand.
He looked at me with cold, slant eyes;
And knelt to the ground: there he died!

Then, all my joy changed to fear,
Or, maybe to 'brother-like' care.
I notice that a crowd had come
To join and share their love as one.

I told them how I was happy
That they had come to share with me.
Without word or smile, sneeze or cough,
They rushed on me and carried me off!
The first day here, I raged and cried.
To break the bars I even tried.
Then I thought: "What will I do…?
Go search out the selected few?"
I soon relaxed so they could go;
And wondered how I might them show:
That what I saw was really there,
That no man has color to bear.

During the night, I came to see
That brown and white and red must be,
As a challenge to those who claim:
"Christ the Picture, we as the Frame."
Surely enough, before morn had come,
I knew full well what I had done:
I had let my heart's vision be
The only sight my eyes could see.

I wanted to tell the world
The truth about God's earthly pearl.
I wanted all to feel as I:

To God as son, to Satan as spy.
I wanted to tell that pigment dies
Shortly after Death claims the eyes—
That when the Ghost of God's with us,
Everything glows, from white to rust!

But now I sit, locked in this cage,
Unable to reach fool or sage,
These iron hearts have formed a cell,
A private world in which I dwell.
But within, I know there're others—
Cages like this that shut off brothers.
So, have no fear, my friend or foe;
For I know now why colors show.

Let's look, again, at the Holy Bible on the subject of racism. In my best searches, my finding is one verse—somewhere to be relocated—where one could interpret the statement as a repudiation of slavery as an acceptable human relationship. So what? You ask? So, what does that say to you, to your world view of humanity and man's responsible relation to man; and man's relationship to God…and God's relationship to man? And, how such a relationship is explained to our children—and how it is reconciled among us adults?

Reports are that there are more slaves of various kinds in 2016 than there ever were at any given time in the history of mankind. What does that truth say about the notion of brotherhood and the tenants of the equality of humankind, and what implications does it have for political perspectives and lofty declarations of human values and entitlements and opportunities to embrace life, liberty, and the pursuit of happiness?

Depending upon the source of the information, millions upon millions of human beings live as slaves every day of your life and of my life. This fact is one to remember, for it is the history out of which the *N-WORD* comes. Consider these forms of human bondage (without military and political imprisonment; local political confinements, human isolations and the world of arrests, detentions, penal constraints and crimes of kidnapping), not to mention the prison systems throughout the world. Names are given to categories of slavery in the world: bonded labor, forced labor, sex trafficking, domestic servitude, child labor, forced marriage, expired and willfully extended indentured servitude, and the arena of mental servitude.

It is estimated that some twenty-two million people in the world are trapped in some form of slavery today in 2016, and most of them are children, detained as sex slaves. One thing for sure: slavery is not an American creation. It existed elsewhere and was brought here, but not before the 15th Century. Albeit, hostile relationships existed between and among aborigine black people (with thick lips, flat noses, kinky hair, blackish-brown skin) who are basic inhabitants of all earthly land masses; but, nothing was so formalized or populated to be designated as a slave-master connection.

"Enough is enough." This expression carries powerful and prophetic guidance for those touched by some new motivation or subtle wisdom. I believe it is time now to look at What Can We Do? Or, what Shall we do? Even, how can we best do it (whatever "it" is)? Let me suggest some possible answers: One, we can come to know—really and truly KNOW the phenomenon we so glibly deny and resist (as if we have been or are being wrongly accused, if not smeared unfairly and disproportionately). First, you need to be serious. You have to declare yourself a racist, even if an unintentional racist, unconditionally and without recourse or exception.

Start with who you are, with where you are. While we cannot help being who we are, we are not "all the same." Some of us do quite well moving away from our racist heritage and endowments. So, denial is not an option. What we want to embrace is a commitment to mitigate the reoccurring pain and suffering racism tends to foster. Not an easy task! Not even a task. What we are talking about here is *new birth*, a commitment to a growing joint effort to significantly reduce the presence of racism in our lives. We are talking about a commitment to a re-birth, what the Bible refers to as being *born again*! This is the kind of consciousness that will move us away from increased pain and suffering; separation and estrangement; public, private, police, political, and commercial violence and from economic injustice.

In case you are still defending your non-racist good name, let me remind you of what the issues are: 1) Our racist American society (history and preference) makes us all racists. If you reject this statement, then my response to you is: Nigga, please! 2) Functioning in competitive associations, racism manipulates equity. If you argue otherwise, I say to you: Nigga, please! 3) 500 years of the horrors of slavery will not go away next week, or when Congress is next in session. Racism is here to stay: until enough of us are determined that Enough is Enough! If you see a faster way—leaving out the reshaping of the human soul, I would say to you: Nigga, please! And each time my salutation is simply: "Please be realistic...."

And there is a lot we (collectively) can do, even though we may have to start as smart individuals. Individuals who have the vision to see the Promised Land, that place and time when we laugh together, in safety and in peace, recognizing our historic racist behaviors and we acknowledge them. We suck up our pride and reinforce our commitment to work harder to become new persons, persons less controlled and manipulated by our unavoidable legacy of racism—social capital racism and social capital consequences.

One question at this point: Is there still someone who believes she or he is not a RACIST? Can you imagine an army of journalists who editorialize 500 years of the vilest of inhuman conduct, only to conclude (some *intellectual bullshit*) that proposes to be logically conceived, constructed, and presented? But, we must still respect our journalists, as we must our clergy! How will ministers, priests, reverends, pastors, rabbis, missionaries, and every other title of religious leader teach how the Holy Bible supports a man's absolute yearning for freedom (the right to life, liberty, and the pursuit of happiness)? And how will they settle the question—once for all—"Does the Holy

Bible absolutely reject the practice of slavery?" Whatever they answer, there remains one question: Why does racism continue to evolve, even some five hundred years later?

SECTION SIX

"A Surgical Look at One Journalist"

Writing in *The Philadelphia Trumpet* magazine, Gerald Flurry's article is entitled: "America Faces an Explosion of Racial Violence" (September, 2016, page one). The title itself evokes, perhaps, a wide-spread fear among some people—black and white. This approach to commentary about RACISM in America is not uncommon, unfortunately. It is much too easy to play on the survival instincts of large numbers of people; and that heightens potential fears. Gerald Flurry's treatment purports to point out racist aspects and foundations of comments, presumptions, critical omissions, and inability to see essential dynamics.

To better help you understand my point of view, I will use an analogy. Let us compare something we call RACISM with the air we breathe. All of us must inhale and exhale this air. And, we do just that. The proof is in the pudding: we all survive; we exist, almost by virtue of the racism we breathe. Now, comparing RACISM to an absolute requirement of life in America, we look at his article on "pending RACIAL violence" and we will take note of the elements of RACISM as they appear.

Even experienced journalists are not exempt from being RACISTS—none of us is. Let's look at the author's preliminary conclusions: First, he writes: *"Assassinations of police officers in Dallas and Baton Rouge mark a dangerous escalation of race hatred."* First, Flurry reminds us our armed protectors are being attacked; and that this force which we will need to protect us from the *explosion of racial violence* is being diminished by "a dangerous escalation of racial hatred." All of this *information* is given to the reader, even before the first paragraph of the article is presented. At line one, I ask: "Where else can the article, itself, lead?"

Hold on, though; remember, there were two initial conclusions. Let's look at the second one: *"America's highest ranking leaders are fueling the problem."* How awful! Does Gerald Flurry mean (since black people have leaders and white people have representatives) the BLACK PRESIDENT is out and about, fueling the problem, and thus, escalating the presence of racial hatred in American society?

Remember the racism air we all must breathe in order to survive in American society? First, Mr. Flurry shows his own racism by his announcement of a "dangerous escalation of racial hatred." What if all the assassins were white? Or, if all of the murdered policemen where black? Next, he disrespects The Office of the Presidency—and the President of the United States of America—and dares write, put into print, and distributes to a worldwide audience, his personally biased and racist ramblings about a dynamic, 500-year-old cancer that eats at all of us.

What Gerald Flurry has to realize is that being a racist is okay; it's just not okay to remain one—not for him, for you, or for me. We who want to save our country, and ourselves, will have to come face to face with our mirror images, and then commit our corporate energies to seeing who we are and who we want to become. And, we have to make *a one-hundred-year-commitment* to fairly share our common reality.

Flurry went farther: he even laid blame on the American people for electing that "highest ranking leader," who is "fueling" the people-police violence (as investigation results and due process-not guilty decisions confirm). Mr. Flurry shows little cognizance that investigations are conducted by well-meaning racists; and jurors who view evidence and draw conclusions are racists, no matter how they vote. The issue going forward is not who we are now, but about who we are determined to become! And, for the record: a strong police force IS NOT our best option going forward. Our better option is a strong and committed community of Americans who want to live together in an equal-opportunity environment.

It is a long article and I could go on and on in greater detail, pointing out examples of Gerald Flurry's remarks that confirm he is racist (like the rest of us!), and like many other journalists remains unbelievably naïve . We are all racists—remember? We all breathe and exist sharing the same *racist air*. It is our history here in America. We are 500 years into our race-based co-existence. Sooner than later, we will need to own up. Our hope for the future lies in our becoming truly aware today.

Let's look at two other statements by Flurry. In the second part of the article ("Building Racial Tension"), Flurry writes: "To call somebody a racist is one of the ugliest accusations you can make in America today." He adds: "To falsely accuse people of racism routinely is a serious problem." That "serious problem" is of the feared consequences of "this slippery slope that is moving America toward a race war and rule by dictatorship or tyranny."

Racism—again—is relating value judgments to people based on their racial identity, history, or presumed ethnicity (since that has been our way of life for some 500 years now). I believe it is accurate to speculate that all Americans are racists, whether we know it or not. Once we come to know we are, we can make decisions about what kind of future we want to be moving toward.

Essentially, we can one day come to a point in our social awareness that we realize and acknowledge we are sons and daughters of a tradition that evolved by fierce focus on race: all aspects of life favored whites, at the expense of blacks; and society evolved as a race-focused culture. That standard of co-existence continues, favoring whites and disfavoring blacks. As a nation, America would do well to put a huge dent in racial disparity within the next hundred years. How we handle the 100-year gestation period is critical to the survival of our promising democracy. I pray we come together, with commitment, and do what is right for each other. I pray.

CONCLUDING REMARKS

My final prayer: that women and men come together at the commitment level, and we work together and with our children to fess up, make a better decision about the kind of society we want to co-exist in. We can do this. There are multiple rewards in store for us as we succeed. But, first, we must make a clear and contagious beginning; and we must do it where we are, as we are, with whoever is racially distinguishable. And, if we don't see such people in our daily lives, then we must go out and connect with them, or change our personal environments to include them; and we must share our passion to survive...together, as sisters and brothers...under God, and/or under the flag of the United States of America. And, this plea primarily addresses our racism issue.

A LAST THOUGHT

This generation of men
defend through searching:
a die-hard faith in a
free yester-mother; but
Wise men know it, as fools feel
it in their foolish ways:
In this ambiguous world,
Neither is freer than the other.
True freedom is never singular;
it is always plural.
Unless a man fools himself,
his freedom needs his brother.
No man is a free man, en-
tire unto himself for
Each man's freedom is bound
to the freedom of another.

ABOUT THE AUTHOR

Dr. Henry L.N. Anderson grew up in Savannah but left GA at the age of 16, headed for a new life in Philadelphia, Pennsylvania where he graduated from Benjamin Franklin High School for Boys, winning a Board of Education four-year scholarship to college.

He entered Earlham College in Richmond, Indiana as a pre-medical student, transferred and graduated from Cheyney University of Pennsylvania as a teacher. He was accepted as a candidate for the Episcopal priesthood by the Divinity School at Yale University, New Haven, CT., where in 1958, he met and became life-long friends with Rev. Dr. Martin Luther King, Jr. Arriving in Los Angeles on September 7, 1959 he later formed Western Publishers, Ltd., and was the first publisher ever to accept, finance, and publish a book (*She Walks in Beauty, a novel*) written by the famous 'Negro Historian,' J. A. Rogers. In 1960, he self-published his own first Small Book™, *You and Race: A Christian Reflects*. He later had a private audience with Mother Teresa in Calcutta, India, when she described

Jesus' life mission in five words: *"Jesus did it unto them."*

In 1974, with some twenty family, friends, and students he co-founded *City University Los Angeles* (CULA®), in response to the Carnegie Commission's Report that American higher education needed a system that would afford mature adults the opportunity to spend *less time and more options* for completing a college degree.

In 1986, he was introduced to Natural Hygiene and became a vegetarian, later elevating to a fruitarian, and published his first book on "The science of healthful living" in the same year. Now, some fifteen published books later, he gives us The *N-WORD* Revisited. Still jogging three miles, at least twice a week, working out and pursuing a Natural Hygiene lifestyle, he celebrates his 83rd birthday on May 23, 2017, with no medical complaints. When asked about his personal physician and medical treatments, he jokingly quips, "All my doctors are dead!"

SUGGESTED REFERENCES

– Anderson, Henry L. N., *No Use Cryin'* (a novel about interracial love in Georgia)
– Allport, Gordon, *The Nature of Prejudice*
– Adams, James T., Epic *of America*
– Fast, Howard, *Freedom Road*
– Golden, Harry, *Only in America*
– Herskovits, Merville J., *The Myth of the Negro Past*
– Moore, George H*., Notes on the History of Slavery in Massachusetts*, New York, 1866.
– King, Martin Luther, *Stride Toward Freedom*
– Cash, W. J., *Mind of the South*
– Frazier, E. Franklin, *Black Bourgeoisie*
– Paton, Alan, *Cry, the Beloved Country*
– Hansberry, Lorraine*, A Raisin in the Sun*
– Wright, Richard, *Black Boy*
– Pope, Liston, *Kingdom Beyond Caste*
– Smith, Lillian, *Killers of the Dream*
– Shute, Nevile, *Round the Bend*
– Benedict, Ruth, *Patterns of Culture*
– Lee, Norhm, Ph.D., *Relationships, Truth, and Now*
– Dollard, John, *Caste and Class in a Southern Town*
– Anderson, Henry L. N., *Revolutionary Urban Teaching*
– Anderson, Henry L. N., *African, Born in America*
– Fry, T. C., *The Great A.I.D.S. Hoax*
– Anderson, Henry L. N., *Hidden Hand* (cancer and social class)

WHAT'S NEXT?

BEYOND RACISM: SEXISM

How long is it going to take for men to shake women by the hand, and not "grab them by the p---y", as stated by Donald J. Trump, who, on January 20, 2017, was sworn in as President of the United States of America. A statement so sexist, it reduces every woman around the world to a commodity, to a thing; put here on earth for the entertainment and pleasure of man, "the superior creature."

Have we heard this concept before…?

www.ingramcontent.com/pod-product-compliance
Lightning Source LLC
Chambersburg PA
CBHW031608040426
42452CB00006B/448